Connected Mathematics 2

W9-BRW-312

Thinking With Mathematical Models

Linear and Inverse Variation

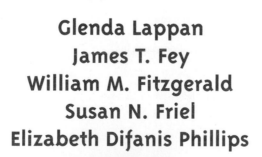

Glenda Lappan

James T. Fey

William M. Fitzgerald

Susan N. Friel

Elizabeth Difanis Phillips

PEARSON

Prentice Hall

Boston, Massachusetts
Upper Saddle River, New Jersey

Connected Mathematics™ was developed at Michigan State University with financial support from the Michigan State University Office of the Provost, Computing and Technology, and the College of Natural Science.

This material is based upon work supported by the National Science Foundation under Grant No. MDR 9150217 and Grant No. ESI 9986372. Opinions expressed are those of the authors and not necessarily those of the Foundation.

The Michigan State University authors and administration have agreed that all MSU royalties arising from this publication will be devoted to purposes supported by the MSU Mathematics Education Enrichment Fund.

Acknowledgments appear on page 69, which constitutes an extension of this copyright page.

Pearson Prentice Hall™ is a trademark of Pearson Education, Inc.
Pearson® is a registered trademark of Pearson plc.
Prentice Hall® is a registered trademark of Pearson Education, Inc.

ExamView® is a registered trademark of FSCreations, Inc.

Connected Mathematics™ is a trademark of Michigan State University.

ISBN 0-13-165647-3
5 6 7 8 9 10   09 08 07

Authors of Connected Mathematics

(from left to right) Glenda Lappan, Betty Phillips, Susan Friel, Bill Fitzgerald, Jim Fey

Glenda Lappan is a University Distinguished Professor in the Department of Mathematics at Michigan State University. Her research and development interests are in the connected areas of students' learning of mathematics and mathematics teachers' professional growth and change related to the development and enactment of K–12 curriculum materials.

James T. Fey is a Professor of Curriculum and Instruction and Mathematics at the University of Maryland. His consistent professional interest has been development and research focused on curriculum materials that engage middle and high school students in problem-based collaborative investigations of mathematical ideas and their applications.

William M. Fitzgerald *(Deceased)* was a Professor in the Department of Mathematics at Michigan State University. His early research was on the use of concrete materials in supporting student learning and led to the development of teaching materials for laboratory environments. Later he helped develop a teaching model to support student experimentation with mathematics.

Susan N. Friel is a Professor of Mathematics Education in the School of Education at the University of North Carolina at Chapel Hill. Her research interests focus on statistics education for middle-grade students and, more broadly, on teachers' professional development and growth in teaching mathematics K–8.

Elizabeth Difanis Phillips is a Senior Academic Specialist in the Mathematics Department of Michigan State University. She is interested in teaching and learning mathematics for both teachers and students. These interests have led to curriculum and professional development projects at the middle school and high school levels, as well as projects related to the teaching and learning of algebra across the grades.

CMP2 Development Staff

Teacher Collaborator in Residence
Yvonne Grant
Michigan State University

Production and Field Site Manager
Lisa Keller
Michigan State University

Administrative Assistant
Judith Martus Miller
Michigan State University

Technical and Editorial Support
Brin Keller, Peter Lappan, Jim Laser,
Michael Masterson, Stacey Miceli

Assessment Team
June Bailey and **Debra Sobko** (Apollo Middle School, Rochester, New York), **George Bright** (University of North Carolina, Greensboro), **Gwen Ranzau Campbell** (Sunrise Park Middle School, White Bear Lake, Minnesota), **Holly DeRosia, Kathy Dole,** and **Teri Keusch** (Portland Middle School, Portland, Michigan), **Mary Beth Schmitt** (Traverse City East Junior High School, Traverse City, Michigan), **Genni Steele** (Central Middle School, White Bear Lake, Minnesota), **Jacqueline Stewart** (Okemos, Michigan), **Elizabeth Tye** (Magnolia Junior High School, Magnolia, Arkansas)

Development Assistants
At Lansing Community College *Undergraduate Assistant:* **James Brinegar**

At Michigan State University *Graduate Assistants:* **Dawn Berk, Emily Bouck, Bulent Buyukbozkirli, Kuo-Liang Chang, Christopher Danielson, Srinivasa Dharmavaram, Deb Johanning, Kelly Rivette, Sarah Sword, Tat Ming Sze, Marie Turini, Jeffrey Wanko;** *Undergraduate Assistants:* **Daniel Briggs, Jeffrey Chapin, Jade Corsé, Elisha Hardy, Alisha Harold, Elizabeth Keusch, Julia Letoutchaia, Karen Loeffler, Brian Oliver, Carl Oliver, Evonne Pedawi, Lauren Rebrovich**

At the University of Maryland *Graduate Assistants:* **Kim Harris Bethea, Kara Karch**

At the University of North Carolina (Chapel Hill) *Graduate Assistants:* **Mark Ellis, Trista Stearns;** *Undergraduate Assistant:* **Daniel Smith**

Advisory Board for CMP2

Thomas Banchoff
Professor of Mathematics
Brown University
Providence, Rhode Island

Anne Bartel
Mathematics Coordinator
Minneapolis Public Schools
Minneapolis, Minnesota

Hyman Bass
Professor of Mathematics
University of Michigan
Ann Arbor, Michigan

Joan Ferrini-Mundy
Associate Dean of the College of
Natural Science; Professor
Michigan State University
East Lansing, Michigan

James Hiebert
Professor
University of Delaware
Newark, Delaware

Susan Hudson Hull
Charles A. Dana Center
University of Texas
Austin, Texas

Michele Luke
Mathematics Curriculum
Coordinator
West Junior High
Minnetonka, Minnesota

Kay McClain
Assistant Professor of
Mathematics Education
Vanderbilt University
Nashville, Tennessee

Edward Silver
Professor; Chair of Educational
Studies
University of Michigan
Ann Arbor, Michigan

Judith Sowder
Professor Emerita
San Diego State University
San Diego, California

Lisa Usher
Mathematics Resource Teacher
California Academy of
Mathematics and Science
San Pedro, California

Field Test Sites for CMP2

During the development of the revised edition of *Connected Mathematics* (CMP2), more than 100 classroom teachers have field-tested materials at 49 school sites in 12 states and the District of Columbia. This classroom testing occurred over three academic years (2001 through 2004), allowing careful study of the effectiveness of each of the 24 units that comprise the program. A special thanks to the students and teachers at these pilot schools.

Arkansas

Magnolia Public Schools
Kittena Bell*, Judith Trowell*; *Central Elementary School:* Maxine Broom, Betty Eddy, Tiffany Fallin, Bonnie Flurry, Carolyn Monk, Elizabeth Tye; *Magnolia Junior High School:* Monique Bryan, Ginger Cook, David Graham, Shelby Lamkin

Colorado

Boulder Public Schools
Nevin Platt Middle School: Judith Koenig

St. Vrain Valley School District, Longmont
Westview Middle School: Colleen Beyer, Kitty Canupp, Ellie Decker*, Peggy McCarthy, Tanya deNobrega, Cindy Payne, Ericka Pilon, Andrew Roberts

District of Columbia

Capitol Hill Day School: Ann Lawrence

Georgia

University of Georgia, Athens
Brad Findell

Madison Public Schools
Morgan County Middle School: Renee Burgdorf, Lynn Harris, Nancy Kurtz, Carolyn Stewart

Maine

Falmouth Public Schools
Falmouth Middle School: Donna Erikson, Joyce Hebert, Paula Hodgkins, Rick Hogan, David Legere, Cynthia Martin, Barbara Stiles, Shawn Towle*

Michigan

Portland Public Schools
Portland Middle School: Mark Braun, Holly DeRosia, Kathy Dole*, Angie Foote, Teri Keusch, Tammi Wardwell

Traverse City Area Public Schools
Bertha Vos Elementary: Kristin Sak; *Central Grade School:* Michelle Clark; Jody Meyers; *Eastern Elementary:* Karrie Tufts; *Interlochen Elementary:* Mary McGee-Cullen; *Long Lake Elementary:* Julie Faulkner*, Charlie Maxbauer, Katherine Sleder; *Norris Elementary:* Hope Slanaker; *Oak Park Elementary:* Jessica Steed; *Traverse Heights Elementary:* Jennifer Wolfert; *Westwoods Elementary:* Nancy Conn; *Old Mission Peninsula School:* Deb Larimer; *Traverse City East Junior High:* Ivanka Berkshire, Ruthanne Kladder, Jan Palkowski, Jane Peterson, Mary Beth Schmitt; *Traverse City West Junior High:* Dan Fouch*, Ray Fouch

Sturgis Public Schools
Sturgis Middle School: Ellen Eisele

Minnesota

Burnsville School District 191
Hidden Valley Elementary: Stephanie Cin, Jane McDevitt

Hopkins School District 270
Alice Smith Elementary: Sandra Cowing, Kathleen Gustafson, Martha Mason, Scott Stillman; *Eisenhower Elementary:* Chad Bellig, Patrick Berger, Nancy Glades, Kye Johnson, Shane Wasserman, Victoria Wilson; *Gatewood Elementary:* Sarah Ham, Julie Kloos, Janine Pung, Larry Wade; *Glen Lake Elementary:* Jacqueline Cramer, Kathy Hering, Cecelia Morris,

Robb Trenda; *Katherine Curren Elementary:* Diane Bancroft, Sue DeWit, John Wilson; *L. H. Tanglen Elementary:* Kevin Athmann, Lisa Becker, Mary LaBelle, Kathy Rezac, Roberta Severson; *Meadowbrook Elementary:* Jan Gauger, Hildy Shank, Jessica Zimmerman; *North Junior High:* Laurel Hahn, Kristin Lee, Jodi Markuson, Bruce Mestemacher, Laurel Miller, Bonnie Rinker, Jeannine Salzer, Sarah Shafer, Cam Stottler; *West Junior High:* Alicia Beebe, Kristie Earl, Nobu Fujii, Pam Georgetti, Susan Gilbert, Regina Nelson Johnson, Debra Lindstrom, Michele Luke*, Jon Sorenson

Minneapolis School District 1
Ann Sullivan K-8 School: Bronwyn Collins; Anne Bartel* (Curriculum and Instruction Office)

Wayzata School District 284
Central Middle School: Sarajane Myers, Dan Nielsen, Tanya Ravenholdt

White Bear Lake School District 624
Central Middle School: Amy Jorgenson, Michelle Reich, Brenda Sammon

New York

New York City Public Schools
IS 89: Yelena Aynbinder, Chi-Man Ng, Nina Rapaport, Joel Spengler, Phyllis Tam*, Brent Wyso; *Wagner Middle School:* Jason Appel, Intissar Fernandez, Yee Gee Get, Richard Goldstein, Irving Marcus, Sue Norton, Bernadita Owens, Jennifer Rehn*, Kevin Yuhas

---

* indicates a Field Test Site Coordinator

Ohio

Talawanda School District, Oxford
Talawanda Middle School: Teresa Abrams, Larry Brock, Heather Brosey, Julie Churchman, Monna Even, Karen Fitch, Bob George, Amanda Klee, Pat Meade, Sandy Montgomery, Barbara Sherman, Lauren Steidl

Miami University
Jeffrey Wanko*

Springfield Public Schools
Rockway School: Jim Mamer

Pennsylvania

Pittsburgh Public Schools
Kenneth Labuskes, Marianne O'Connor, Mary Lynn Raith*; *Arthur J. Rooney Middle School:* David Hairston, Stamatina Mousetis, Alfredo Zangaro; *Frick International Studies Academy:* Suzanne Berry, Janet Falkowski, Constance Finseth, Romika Hodge, Frank Machi; *Reizenstein Middle School:* Jeff Baldwin, James Brautigam, Lorena Burnett, Glen Cobbett, Michael Jordan, Margaret Lazur, Melissa Munnell, Holly Neely, Ingrid Reed, Dennis Reft

Texas

Austin Independent School District
Bedichek Middle School: Lisa Brown, Jennifer Glasscock, Vicki Massey

El Paso Independent School District
Cordova Middle School: Armando Aguirre, Anneliesa Durkes, Sylvia Guzman, Pat Holguin*, William Holguin, Nancy Nava, Laura Orozco, Michelle Peña, Roberta Rosen, Patsy Smith, Jeremy Wolf

Plano Independent School District
Patt Henry, James Wohlgehagen*; *Frankford Middle School:* Mandy Baker, Cheryl Butsch, Amy Dudley, Betsy Eshelman, Janet Greene, Cort Haynes, Kathy Letchworth, Kay Marshall, Kelly McCants, Amy Reck, Judy Scott, Syndy Snyder, Lisa Wang; *Wilson Middle School:* Darcie Bane, Amanda Bedenko, Whitney Evans, Tonelli Hatley, Sarah (Becky) Higgs, Kelly Johnston, Rebecca McElligott, Kay Neuse, Cheri Slocum, Kelli Straight

Washington

Evergreen School District
Shahala Middle School: Nicole Abrahamsen, Terry Coon*, Carey Doyle, Sheryl Drechsler, George Gemma, Gina Helland, Amy Hilario, Darla Lidyard, Sean McCarthy, Tilly Meyer, Willow Neuwelt, Todd Parsons, Brian Pederson, Stan Posey, Shawn Scott, Craig Sjoberg, Lynette Sundstrom, Charles Switzer, Luke Youngblood

Wisconsin

Beaver Dam Unified School District
Beaver Dam Middle School: Jim Braemer, Jeanne Frick, Jessica Greatens, Barbara Link, Dennis McCormick, Karen Michels, Nancy Nichols*, Nancy Palm, Shelly Stelsel, Susan Wiggins

---

* indicates a Field Test Site Coordinator

Reviews of CMP to Guide Development of CMP2

Before writing for CMP2 began or field tests were conducted, the first edition of *Connected Mathematics* was submitted to the mathematics faculties of school districts from many parts of the country and to 80 individual reviewers for extensive comments.

School District Survey Reviews of CMP

Arizona
Madison School District #38 (Phoenix)

Arkansas
Cabot School District, Little Rock School District, Magnolia School District

California
Los Angeles Unified School District

Colorado
St. Vrain Valley School District (Longmont)

Florida
Leon County Schools (Tallahassee)

Illinois
School District #21 (Wheeling)

Indiana
Joseph L. Block Junior High (East Chicago)

Kentucky
Fayette County Public Schools (Lexington)

Maine
Selection of Schools

Massachusetts
Selection of Schools

Michigan
Sparta Area Schools

Minnesota
Hopkins School District

Texas
Austin Independent School District, The El Paso Collaborative for Academic Excellence, Plano Independent School District

Wisconsin
Platteville Middle School

Individual Reviewers of CMP

Arkansas
Deborah Cramer; Robby Frizzell *(Taylor)*; Lowell Lynde *(University of Arkansas, Monticello)*; Leigh Manzer *(Norfork)*; Lynne Roberts *(Emerson High School, Emerson)*; Tony Timms *(Cabot Public Schools)*; Judith Trowell *(Arkansas Department of Higher Education)*

California
José Alcantar *(Gilroy)*; Eugenie Belcher *(Gilroy)*; Marian Pasternack *(Lowman M. S. T. Center, North Hollywood)*; Susana Pezoa *(San Jose)*; Todd Rabusin *(Hollister)*; Margaret Siegfried *(Ocala Middle School, San Jose)*; Polly Underwood *(Ocala Middle School, San Jose)*

Colorado
Janeane Golliher *(St. Vrain Valley School District, Longmont)*; Judith Koenig *(Nevin Platt Middle School, Boulder)*

Florida
Paige Loggins *(Swift Creek Middle School, Tallahassee)*

Illinois
Jan Robinson *(School District #21, Wheeling)*

Indiana
Frances Jackson *(Joseph L. Block Junior High, East Chicago)*

Kentucky
Natalee Feese *(Fayette County Public Schools, Lexington)*

Maine
Betsy Berry *(Maine Math & Science Alliance, Augusta)*

Maryland
Joseph Gagnon *(University of Maryland, College Park)*; Paula Maccini *(University of Maryland, College Park)*

Massachusetts
George Cobb *(Mt. Holyoke College, South Hadley)*; Cliff Kanold *(University of Massachusetts, Amherst)*

Michigan
Mary Bouck *(Farwell Area Schools)*; Carol Dorer *(Slauson Middle School, Ann Arbor)*; Carrie Heaney *(Forsythe Middle School, Ann Arbor)*; Ellen Hopkins *(Clague Middle School, Ann Arbor)*; Teri Keusch *(Portland Middle School, Portland)*; Valerie Mills *(Oakland Schools, Waterford)*; Mary Beth Schmitt *(Traverse City East Junior High, Traverse City)*; Jack Smith *(Michigan State University, East Lansing)*; Rebecca Spencer *(Sparta Middle School, Sparta)*; Ann Marie Nicoll Turner *(Tappan Middle School, Ann Arbor)*; Scott Turner *(Scarlett Middle School, Ann Arbor)*

Minnesota
Margarita Alvarez *(Olson Middle School, Minneapolis)*; Jane Amundson *(Nicollet Junior High, Burnsville)*; Anne Bartel *(Minneapolis Public Schools)*; Gwen Ranzau Campbell *(Sunrise Park Middle School, White Bear Lake)*; Stephanie Cin *(Hidden Valley Elementary, Burnsville)*; Joan Garfield *(University of Minnesota, Minneapolis)*; Gretchen Hall *(Richfield Middle School, Richfield)*; Jennifer Larson *(Olson Middle School, Minneapolis)*; Michele Luke *(West Junior High, Minnetonka)*; Jeni Meyer *(Richfield Junior High, Richfield)*; Judy Pfingsten *(Inver Grove Heights Middle School, Inver Grove Heights)*; Sarah Shafer *(North Junior High, Minnetonka)*; Genni Steele *(Central Middle School, White Bear Lake)*; Victoria Wilson *(Eisenhower Elementary, Hopkins)*; Paul Zorn *(St. Olaf College, Northfield)*

New York
Debra Altenau-Bartolino *(Greenwich Village Middle School, New York)*; Doug Clements *(University of Buffalo)*; Francis Curcio *(New York University, New York)*; Christine Dorosh *(Clinton School for Writers, Brooklyn)*; Jennifer Rehn *(East Side Middle School, New York)*; Phyllis Tam *(IS 89 Lab School, New York)*; Marie Turini *(Louis Armstrong Middle School, New York)*; Lucy West *(Community School District 2, New York)*; Monica Witt *(Simon Baruch Intermediate School 104, New York)*

Pennsylvania
Robert Aglietti *(Pittsburgh)*; Sharon Mihalich *(Pittsburgh)*; Jennifer Plumb *(South Hills Middle School, Pittsburgh)*; Mary Lynn Raith *(Pittsburgh Public Schools)*

Texas
Michelle Bittick *(Austin Independent School District)*; Margaret Cregg *(Plano Independent School District)*; Sheila Cunningham *(Klein Independent School District)*; Judy Hill *(Austin Independent School District)*; Patricia Holguin *(El Paso Independent School District)*; Bonnie McNemar *(Arlington)*; Kay Neuse *(Plano Independent School District)*; Joyce Polanco *(Austin Independent School District)*; Marge Ramirez *(University of Texas at El Paso)*; Pat Rossman *(Baker Campus, Austin)*; Cindy Schimek *(Houston)*; Cynthia Schneider *(Charles A. Dana Center, University of Texas at Austin)*; Uri Treisman *(Charles A. Dana Center, University of Texas at Austin)*; Jacqueline Weilmuenster *(Grapevine-Colleyville Independent School District)*; LuAnn Weynand *(San Antonio)*; Carmen Whitman *(Austin Independent School District)*; James Wohlgehagen *(Plano Independent School District)*

Washington
Ramesh Gangolli *(University of Washington, Seattle)*

Wisconsin
Susan Lamon *(Marquette University, Hales Corner)*; Steve Reinhart *(retired, Chippewa Falls Middle School, Eau Claire)*

Table of Contents

Thinking With Mathematical Models
Linear and Inverse Variation

Thinking With Mathematical Models

Linear and Inverse Variation

How is the thickness of a steel beam or bridge related to its strength? How is the length of a beam or bridge related to its strength?

The equation $c = 4 + 0.10t$ gives the charge c in dollars for renting a paddle boat for t minutes. For how long can you rent a paddle boat if you have $12?

The cost for a group of students to go on an overnight field trip to a nature center is $750. Describe the shape of a graph relating the number of students to the cost per student.

In earlier *Connected Mathematics* units, you explored relationships between variables. You learned to recognize linear relationships from patterns in tables and graphs and to write equations for such relationships. You then used the equations to help you solve problems. As you work through the investigations in this unit, you will enhance your skill in recognizing and analyzing linear relationships. You will also compare linear patterns with nonlinear patterns, focusing on a special type of nonlinear relationship called an *inverse variation*.

You will conduct experiments, analyze the data, and then write equations that summarize, or model, the data patterns. You will then use your equations to make predictions about values beyond and between the data you collected.

The skills you develop in this unit will help you answer questions like those on the facing page.

Mathematical Highlights

Linear and Inverse Variation

In *Thinking With Mathematical Models,* you will model relationships with graphs and equations, and then use your models to analyze situations and solve problems.

You will learn how to:

- Recognize linear and nonlinear patterns in tables and graphs
- Describe data patterns using words and symbols
- Write equations to express patterns appearing in tables, graphs, and problems
- Solve linear equations
- Model situations with inequalities
- Write equations to describe inverse variations
- Use linear and inverse variation equations to solve problems and to make predictions and decisions

As you work on problems in this unit, ask yourself questions about problem situations that involve related variables.

What are the key variables in this situation?

What is the pattern relating the variables?

What kind of equation will express the relationship?

How can I use the equation to answer questions about the relationship?

Investigation 1

Exploring Data Patterns

People in many professions use data and mathematical reasoning to solve problems and make predictions. For example, engineers analyze data from laboratory tests to determine how much weight a bridge can hold. Market researchers use customer survey data to predict demand for new products. Stockbrokers use algebraic formulas to forecast how much their investments will earn over time.

In several previous *Connected Mathematics* units, you used tables, graphs, and equations to explore and describe relationships between variables. In this investigation, you will develop your skill in using these tools to organize data from an experiment, find patterns, and make predictions.

1.1 Testing Bridge Thickness

Many bridges are built with frames of steel beams. Steel is very strong, but any beam will bend or break if you put enough weight on it. The amount of weight a beam can support is related to its thickness, length, and design. To design a bridge, engineers need to understand these relationships.

- How do you think the thickness of a beam is related to its strength? Do you think the relationship is linear?
- What other variables might affect the strength of a bridge?

Engineers often use scale models to test their designs. You can do your own experiments to discover mathematical patterns involved in building bridges.

Instructions for the Bridge-Thickness Experiment

Equipment:

- Two books of the same thickness
- A small paper cup
- About 50 pennies
- Several 11-inch-by-$4\frac{1}{4}$-inch strips of paper

Instructions:

- Start with one of the paper strips. Make a "bridge" by folding up 1 inch on each long side.

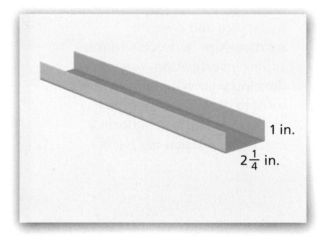

- Suspend the bridge between the books. The bridge should overlap each book by about 1 inch. Place the cup in the center of the bridge.

- Put pennies into the cup, one at a time, until the bridge collapses. Record the number of pennies you added to the cup. This number is the *breaking weight* of the bridge.

- Put two *new* strips of paper together to make a bridge of double thickness. Find the breaking weight for this bridge.

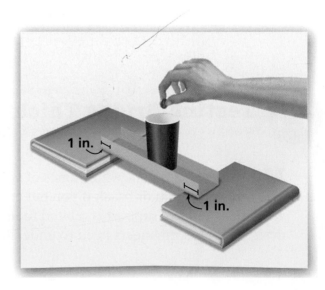

- Repeat this experiment to find the breaking weights of bridges made from three, four, and five strips of paper.

A. Conduct the bridge-thickness experiment to find breaking weights for bridges 1, 2, 3, 4, and 5 layers thick. Record your data in a table.

B. Make a graph of your (*bridge layers, breaking weight*) data.

C. Does the relationship between bridge thickness and breaking weight seem to be linear or nonlinear? How is this shown in the table and graph?

D. Suppose you could split layers of paper in half. What breaking weight would you predict for a bridge 2.5 layers thick? Explain.

E. 1. Predict the breaking weight for a bridge 6 layers thick. Explain your reasoning.

   2. Test your prediction. Explain why results from such tests might not exactly match predictions.

ACE **Homework starts on page 12.**

active math
online

For: Virtual Bridge Experiment
Visit: PHSchool.com
Web Code: apd-1101

In the last problem, you tested paper bridges of various thicknesses. You found that thicker bridges are stronger than thinner bridges. In this problem, you will experiment with paper bridges of various lengths.

How do you think the length of a bridge is related to its strength?

Are longer bridges stronger or weaker than shorter bridges?

You can do an experiment to find out how the length and strength of a bridge are related.

Instructions for the Bridge-Length Experiment

Equipment:

- Two books of the same thickness
- A small paper cup
- About 50 pennies
- $4\frac{1}{4}$-inch-wide strips with lengths 4, 6, 8, 9, and 11 inches

Instructions:

- Make paper bridges from the strips. For each strip, fold up 1 inch on each of the $4\frac{1}{4}$-inch sides.

- Start with the 4-inch bridge. Suspend the bridge between the two books as you did before. The bridge should overlap each book by about 1 inch. Place the paper cup in the center of the bridge.

- Put pennies into the cup, one at a time, until the bridge collapses. Record the number of pennies you added to the cup. As in the first experiment, this number is the breaking weight of the bridge.

- Repeat the experiment to find breaking weights for the other bridges.

Problem 1.2 Finding Patterns and Making Predictions

A. Conduct the bridge-length experiment to find breaking weights for bridges of lengths 4, 6, 8, 9, and 11 inches. Record your data in a table.

B. Make a graph of your data.

C. Describe the relationship between bridge length and breaking weight. How is that relationship shown by patterns in your table and graph?

D. Use your data to predict the breaking weights for bridges of lengths 3, 5, 10, and 12 inches. Explain how you made your predictions.

E. Compare your data from this experiment with the data from the bridge-thickness experiment. How is the relationship between bridge thickness and breaking weight similar to the relationship between bridge length and breaking weight? How is it different?

ACE Homework starts on page 12.

Did You Know?

When designing a bridge, engineers need to consider the *load*, or the amount of weight, the bridge must support. The *dead load* is the weight of the bridge and fixed objects on the bridge. The *live load* is the weight of moving objects on the bridge.

On many city bridges in Europe—such as the famous Ponte Vecchio in Florence, Italy—dead load is very high because tollbooths, apartments, and shops are built right onto the bridge surface. Local ordinances can limit the amount of automobile and rail traffic on a bridge to help control live load.

Suppose a company called Custom Steel Products (CSP for short) provides construction materials to builders. CSP makes beams and staircase frames by attaching 1-foot-long steel rods in the following patterns. CSP will make these materials in any size a builder needs.

CSP Beams

1-foot steel rod

1-foot beam
made from 3 rods

2-foot beam
made from 7 rods

7-foot beam
made from 27 rods

CSP Staircase Frames

1 step
made from 4 rods

2 steps
made from 10 rods

3 steps
made from 18 rods

The manager at CSP needs to know the number of rods required for each design in any size a customer might order. To figure this out, she decides to study a few simple cases. She hopes to find *trends,* or patterns, she can extend to other cases.

Problem 1.3 Extending Patterns

A. 1. Copy and complete the table below to show the number of rods in beams of different lengths. **Hint:** Make drawings of the beams.

CSP Beams

Beam Length (ft)	1	2	3	4	5	6	7	8
Number of Rods	3	7	▪	▪	▪	▪	27	▪

    2. Make a graph of the data in your table.

    3. Describe the pattern of change in the number of rods as the beam length increases.

    4. How is the pattern you described shown in the table? How is it shown in the graph?

    5. How many steel rods are in a beam of length 50 feet? Explain.

B. 1. Copy and complete the table below to show the number of rods in staircase frames with different numbers of steps. **Hint:** Make drawings of the staircase frames.

CSP Staircase Frames

Number of Steps	1	2	3	4	5	6	7	8
Number of Rods	4	10	18	▪	▪	▪	▪	▪

    2. Make a graph of the data in your table.

    3. Describe the pattern of change in the number of rods as the number of steps increases.

    4. How is the pattern you described shown in the table? How is it shown in the graph?

    5. How many steel rods are in a staircase frame with 12 steps?

C. How is the pattern of change in Question A similar to the pattern in Question B? How is it different? Explain how the similarities and differences are shown in the tables and graphs.

D. Compare the patterns of change in this problem with the patterns of change in Problems 1.1 and 1.2. Describe any similarities and differences you find.

ACE Homework starts on page 12.

Applications

1. A group of students conducts the bridge-thickness experiment with construction paper. Their results are shown in this table.

Bridge-Thickness Experiment

Thickness (layers)	1	2	3	4	5	6
Breaking Weight (pennies)	12	20	29	42	52	61

a. Make a graph of the (*thickness, breaking weight*) data. Describe the relationship between thickness and breaking weight.

b. Suppose it is possible to use half-layers of construction paper. What breaking weight would you predict for a bridge 3.5 layers thick? Explain.

c. Predict the breaking weight for a construction-paper bridge 8 layers thick. Explain how you made your prediction.

2. The table shows the maximum weight a crane arm can lift at various distances from its cab. (See the diagram below.)

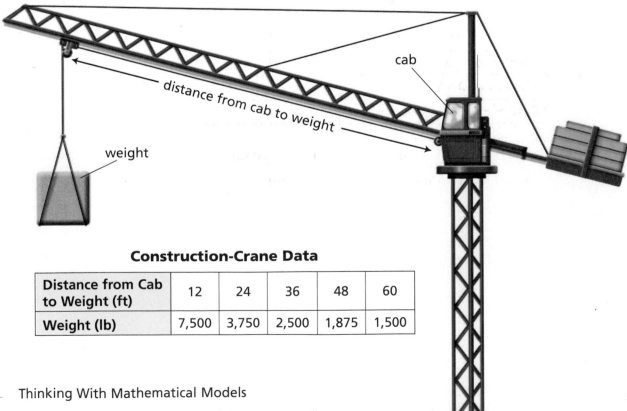

Construction-Crane Data

Distance from Cab to Weight (ft)	12	24	36	48	60
Weight (lb)	7,500	3,750	2,500	1,875	1,500

a. Describe the relationship between distance and weight for the crane.

b. Make a graph of the (*distance, weight*) data. Explain how the graph's shape shows the relationship you described in part (a).

c. Estimate the weight the crane can lift at distances of 18 feet, 30 feet, and 72 feet from the cab.

d. How, if at all, is the crane data similar to the data from the bridge experiments in Problems 1.1 and 1.2?

3. A beam or staircase frame from CSP costs $2.25 for each rod, plus $50 for shipping and handling.

a. Refer to your data for Question A of Problem 1.3. Copy and complete the following table to show the costs for beams of different lengths.

Costs of CSP Beams

Beam Length (ft)	1	2	3	4	5	6	7	8
Number of Rods	3	7	■	■	■	■	27	■
Cost of Beam	■	■	■	■	■	■	■	■

b. Make a graph of the (*beam length, cost*) data.

c. Describe the relationship between beam length and cost.

d. Refer to your data for Question B of Problem 1.3. Copy and complete the following table to show the costs for staircase frames with different numbers of steps.

Costs of CSP Staircase Frames

Number of Steps	1	2	3	4	5	6	7	8
Number of Rods	4	10	18	■	■	■	■	■
Cost of Frame	■	■	■	■	■	■	■	■

e. Make a graph of the (*number of steps, cost*) data.

f. Describe the relationship between the number of steps and the cost.

4. Parts (a)–(f) refer to relationships you have studied in this investigation. Tell whether each relationship is linear.

Homework Help Online

PHSchool.com

For: Help with Exercise 4
Web Code: ape-1104

    a. the relationship between beam length and cost (ACE Exercise 3)

    b. the relationship between the number of steps in a staircase frame and the cost (ACE Exercise 3)

    c. the relationship between bridge thickness and strength (Problem 1.1)

    d. the relationship between bridge length and strength (Problem 1.2)

    e. the relationship between beam length and the number of rods (Problem 1.3)

    f. the relationship between the number of steps in a staircase frame and the number of rods (Problem 1.3)

    g. Compare the patterns of change for all the nonlinear relationships in parts (a)–(f).

5. In many athletic competitions, medals are awarded to top athletes. The medals are often awarded in ceremonies with medal winners standing on special platforms. The sketches show how to make platforms by stacking boxes.

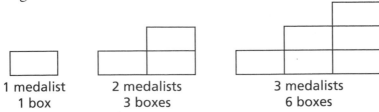

1 medalist
1 box

2 medalists
3 boxes

3 medalists
6 boxes

a. Copy and complete the table below.

Medal Platforms

Number of Medalists	1	2	3	4	5	6	7	8
Number of Boxes	1	3	6	■	■	■	■	■

b. Make a graph of the (*number of medalists, number of boxes*) data.

c. Describe the pattern of change shown in the table and graph.

d. Each box is 1 foot high and 2 feet wide. A red carpet starts 10 feet from the base of the platform, and covers all the risers and steps.

Copy and complete the table below.

Carpet for Platforms

Number of Steps	1	2	3	4	5	6	7	8
Carpet Length (ft)	■	■	■	■	■	■	■	■

e. Make a graph of the (*number of steps, carpet length*) data.

f. Describe the pattern of change in the carpet length as the number of steps increases. Compare this pattern with the pattern in the (*number of medalists, number of boxes*) data.

6. CSP also sells ladder bridges made from 1-foot steel rods arranged to form a row of squares. Below is a 6-foot ladder bridge.

6-foot ladder bridge made from 19 rods

a. Make a table and a graph showing how the number of rods in a ladder bridge is related to length of the bridge.

b. Compare the pattern of change for the ladder bridges with those for the beams and staircase frames in Problem 1.3.

Connections

**A survey of one class at Pioneer Middle School finds that
20 out of 30 students would spend $8 for a school T-shirt.
Use this information for Exercises 7 and 8.**

7. **Multiple Choice** Suppose there are 600 students in the
   school. Based on the survey, how many students do you
   predict would spend $8 for a school T-shirt?

   A. 20   **B.** 200

   C. 300   **D.** 400

8. **Multiple Choice** Suppose there are 450 students in the
   school. Based on the survey, how many students do you
   predict would spend $8 for a school T-shirt?

   F. 20   **G.** 200

   H. 300   **J.** 400

9. Below is a drawing of a rectangle with an area of
   300 square feet.

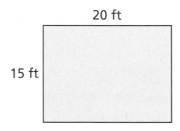
20 ft
15 ft

   a. Make drawings of at least three other rectangles with an area
   of 300 square feet.

   b. What is the width of a rectangle with an area of 300 square feet if
   its length is 1 foot? If its length is 2 feet? If its length is 3 feet?

   c. What is the width of a rectangle with an area of 300 square feet
   and a length of *L* feet?

   d. How does the width of a rectangle change if the length increases,
   but the area remains 300 square feet?

   e. Make a graph of (*width, length*) pairs for a rectangle that give an
   area of 300 square feet. Explain how your graph illustrates your
   answer for part (d).

10. a. The rectangle pictured in Exercise 9 has a perimeter of 70 feet. Make drawings of at least three other rectangles with a perimeter of 70 feet.

b. What is the width of a rectangle with a perimeter of 70 feet if its length is 1 foot? 2 feet? L feet?

c. What is the width of a rectangle with a perimeter of 70 feet if its length is $\frac{1}{2}$ foot? $\frac{3}{2}$ feet?

d. Give the dimensions of rectangles with perimeters of 70 feet and length-to-width ratios of 3 to 4, 4 to 5, and 1 to 1.

e. Suppose the length of a rectangle increases, but the perimeter remains at 70 feet. How does the width change?

f. Make a graph of (*width, length*) pairs that give a perimeter of 70 feet. How does your graph illustrate your answer for part (e)?

11. The 24 students in Ms. Cleary's homeroom are surveyed. They are asked which of several prices they would pay for a ticket to the school fashion show. The results are shown in this table.

Ticket-Price Survey

Ticket Price	$1.00	$1.50	$2.00	$2.50	$3.00	$3.50	$4.00	$4.50
Probable Sales	20	20	18	15	12	10	8	7

a. There are 480 students in the school. Use the data from Ms. Cleary's class to predict ticket sales for the entire school for each price.

b. Use your results from part (a). For each price, find the school's projected income from ticket sales.

c. Which price should the school charge if it wants to earn the maximum possible income?

Tell which graph matches the equation or the set of criteria.

12. $y = 3x + 1$

13. $y = -2x + 2$

14. $y = x - 3$

15. y-intercept = 1; slope = $\frac{1}{2}$

Graph A

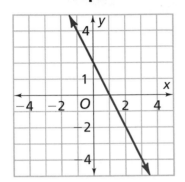

Graph B

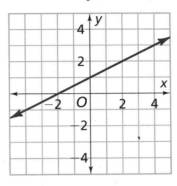

Graph C

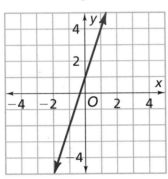

Graph D

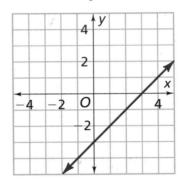

Within each equation, the pouches shown contain the same number of coins. Find the number of coins in each pouch. Explain your method.

16.

17.

18. Refer to Exercises 16 and 17.

  a. For each exercise, write an equation to represent the situation. Let x represent the number of coins in a pouch.

  b. Solve each equation. Explain the steps in your solutions.

  c. Compare your strategies with those you used in Exercises 16 and 17.

Solve each equation for x.

Go Online
PHSchool.com

For: Multiple-Choice Skills Practice

Web Code: apa-1154

19. $3x + 4 = 10$

20. $6x + 3 = 4x + 11$

21. $6x - 3 = 11$

22. $-3x + 5 = 7$

23. $4x - \frac{1}{2} = 8$

24. $\frac{x}{2} - 4 = -5$

25. $3x + 3 = -2x - 12$

26. $\frac{x}{4} - 4 = \frac{3x}{4} - 6$

For Exercises 27–29, tell whether the statement is *true* or *false*. Explain your reasoning.

27. $6(12 - 5) > 50$

28. $3 \cdot 5 - 4 > 6$

29. $10 - 5 \cdot 4 > 0$

30. You will need two sheets of 8.5- by 11-inch paper and some scrap paper.

  a. Roll one sheet of paper to make a cylinder 11 inches high. Overlap the edges very slightly and tape them together. Make bases for the cylinder by tracing the circles on the ends of the cylinder, cutting out the tracings, and taping them in place.

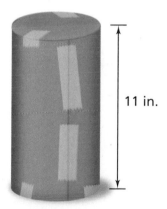

11 in.

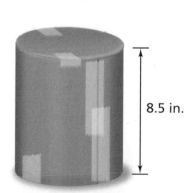

8.5 in.

  b. Roll the other sheet of paper to make a cylinder 8.5 inches high. Make bases as you did in part (a).

  c. Do the cylinders appear to have the same surface area (including the bases)? If not, which has the greater surface area?

  d. Suppose you start with two identical rectangular sheets of paper which are *not* 8.5 by 11 inches. You make two cylinders as you did before. Which cylinder will have the greater surface area, the taller cylinder or the shorter one? How do you know?

31. The volume of the cone in the drawing at right is $\frac{1}{3}(28)\pi$. What are some possible radius and height measurements for the cone?

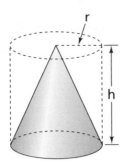

Extensions

32. Study the patterns in this table. Note that the numbers in the *x* column may not be consecutive after *x* = 6.

x	p	q	y	z
1	1	1	2	1
2	4	8	4	$\frac{1}{2}$
3	9	27	8	$\frac{1}{3}$
4	16	64	16	$\frac{1}{4}$
5	25	125	32	$\frac{1}{5}$
6	■	■	■	■
■	■	■	1,024	■
■	■	■	2,048	■
■	■	1,728	■	■
n	■	■	■	■

a. Use the patterns in the first several rows to find the missing values.

b. Are any of the patterns linear? Explain.

33. The table gives data for a group of middle school students.

Data for Middle School Students

Student	Name Length	Height (cm)	Foot Length (cm)
Thomas Petes	11	126	23
Michelle Hughes	14	117	21
Shoshana White	13	112	17
Deborah Locke	12	127	21
Tonya Stewart	12	172	32
Richard Mudd	11	135	22
Tony Tung	8	130	20
Janice Vick	10	134	21
Bobby King	9	156	29
Kathleen Boylan	14	164	28

a. Make a graph of the (*name length, height*) data, a graph of the (*name length, foot length*) data, and a graph of the (*height, foot length*) data.

b. Look at the graphs you made in part (a). Which seem to show linear relationships? Explain.

c. Estimate the average height-to-foot-length ratio. That is, how many "feet" tall is the typical student in the table?

d. Which student has the greatest height-to-foot-length ratio? Which student has the least height-to-foot-length ratio?

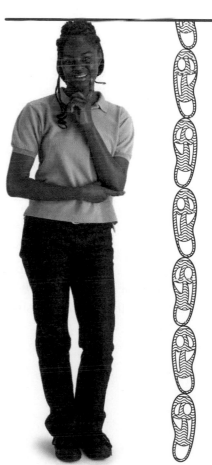

34. A staircase is a prism. This is easier to see if the staircase is viewed from a different perspective. In the prism below, the small squares on the top each have an area of 1 square unit.

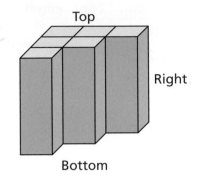

Top

Right

Bottom

a. Sketch the base of the prism. What is the area of the base?

b. Rashid is trying to draw a *net* (flat pattern) that will fold up to form the staircase prism. Below is the start of his drawing. Finish Rashid's drawing and give the surface area of the entire staircase. **Hint:** You may want to draw your net on grid paper and then cut it out and fold it to check.

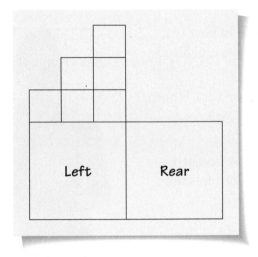

Left   Rear

c. Suppose the prism had six stairs instead of three. Assume each stair is the same width as those in the prism above. Is the surface area of this six-stair prism twice that of the three-stair prism? Explain.

Mathematical Reflections 1

In this investigation, you used tables and graphs to represent relationships between variables and to make predictions. These questions will help you summarize what you have learned.

Think about your answers to these questions. Discuss your ideas with other students and your teacher. Then write a summary of your findings in your notebook.

You can represent a relationship between variables with a table, a graph, or a description in words.

1. What are the advantages and disadvantages of each representation for finding patterns and making predictions?

2. How can you decide from a table whether a relationship is linear?

3. How can you decide from a graph whether a relationship is linear?

Investigation 2

Linear Models and Equations

Organizing and displaying the data from an experiment or survey can help you spot trends and make predictions. When the data show a linear trend, you can find a graph and equation to *model* the relationship between the variables. You can then use the model to make predictions about values between and beyond the data values.

When you make a model to represent a mathematical relationship, examine your model and ask

For what interval of values is the model likely to be reasonably accurate?

2.1 Linear Models

The First State Bridge-Painting Company is often asked to bid on painting projects. It usually gets the contract if it offers the lowest price. However, it needs to make sure the bid is high enough that the company will make a reasonable profit.

First State is preparing a bid for a bridge-painting project. The company looks at its records for previous projects. It finds information about four bridges with similar designs.

First State Bridge-Painting Costs		
Bridge Number	Length (ft)	Painting Cost
1	100	$18,000
2	200	$37,000
3	300	$48,000
4	400	$66,000

The First State cost estimators plot the data. The points fall in a nearly linear pattern. They draw a line that fits the pattern well. The line is a **mathematical model** for the relationship between bridge length and painting cost. A mathematical model approximates a data pattern.

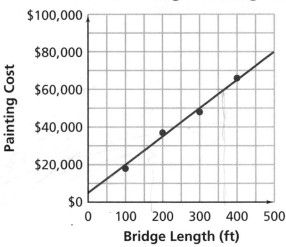

First State Bridge-Painting Costs

Getting Ready for **Problem** 2.1

A mathematical model can be used to make predictions about values between and beyond the data points.

- How do you think the cost estimators decided where to draw the line?
- Is the line a reasonable model for these data?
- What information does the model give that the points alone do not?
- What questions could you answer using the model?
- What information do you need to write an equation for the line?

Problem 2.1 **Linear Models**

A. 1. Write an equation for the line that models the data.

    2. Use the line or the equation to estimate painting costs for similar bridges that are

        a. 175 feet long   **b.** 280 feet long

    3. Use the line or the equation to estimate lengths of similar bridges for which the painting costs are

        a. $10,000   **b.** $60,000

B. First State is also bidding on a different type of bridge. It has records for three similar bridges.

First State Bridge-Painting Costs

Bridge Number	Length (ft)	Painting Cost
3	150	$50,000
4	300	$80,000
5	500	$140,000

1. Plot these data points. Draw a line that models the pattern in the data points.

2. Write an equation for your line.

3. Use your equation or line to estimate the painting cost for a similar bridge that is 200 feet long.

4. Use your equation or line to estimate the length of a similar bridge that costs $100,000 to paint.

ACE Homework starts on page 33.

2.2 Equations for Linear Relationships

Cars and trucks are an important part of American life and culture. There are nearly 200 million licensed drivers and 140 million registered passenger cars in the United States. To help people keep their cars clean, many cities have self-service car washes.

At most self-service car washes, the charge for washing a car and the company's profit depend on the time the customer spends using the car wash. To run such a business efficiently, it helps to have equations relating these key variables.

Getting Ready for Problem 2.2

- Sudzo Wash and Wax charges customers $0.75 per minute to wash a car. Write an equation that relates the total charge c to the amount of time t in minutes.

- Pat's Power Wash charges $2.00 per car to cover the cost of cleaning supplies, plus $0.49 per minute for the use of water sprayers and vacuums. Write an equation for the total charge c for any car-wash time t.

- U-Wash-It charges $10 for each car. The business owners estimate that it costs them $0.60 per minute to provide soap, water, and vacuums for a car. Write an equation for the profit p U-Wash-It earns if a customer spends t minutes washing a car.

- Explain what the numbers and variables in each equation represent.

- What questions can your equations help you answer?

A. The Squeaky Clean Car Wash charges by the minute. This table shows the charges for several different times.

Squeaky Clean Car Wash Charges

Time (min)	5	10	15	20	25
Charge	$8	$13	$18	$23	$28

1. Explain how you know the relationship is linear.

2. What are the slope and *y*-intercept of the line that represents the data?

3. Write an equation relating charge *c* to time *t* in minutes.

B. Euclid's Car Wash displays its charges as a graph. Write an equation for the charge plan at Euclid's. Describe what the variables and numbers in your equation tell you about the situation.

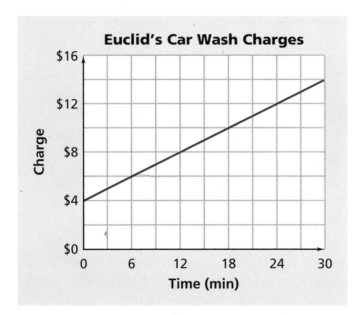

C. Below are two receipts from Super Clean Car Wash. Assume the relationship between charge c and time used t is linear.

SUPER CLEAN
Car Wash
Date: 3-14-05
Start time: 01:55 pm
Stop time: 02:05 pm
Charge: $7.00

SUPER CLEAN
Car Wash
Date: 4-04-05
Start time: 09:30 am
Stop time: 09:50 am
Charge: $12.00

    1. Each receipt represents a point (t, c) on the line. Find the coordinates of the two points.

    2. What are the slope and y-intercept of the line?

    3. Write an equation relating c and t.

D. Write an equation for the line with slope -3 that passes through the point $(4, 3)$.

E. Write an equation for the line with points $(4, 5)$ and $(6, 9)$.

F. Suppose you want to write an equation of the form $y = mx + b$ to represent a linear relationship. What is your strategy if you are given

    1. a description of the relationship in words?

    2. two or more (x, y) values or a table of (x, y) values?

    3. a graph showing points with coordinates?

ACE   **Homework starts on page 33.**

2.3 Solving Linear Equations

Sandy's Boat House rents canoes. The equation $c = 0.15t + 2.50$ gives the charge c in dollars for renting a canoe for t minutes.

Getting Ready for Problem 2.3

- Explain what the numbers in the equation $c = 0.15t + 2.50$ tell you about the situation.

- Rashida and Serena apply for jobs at Sandy's. The manager tests them with three questions.

  What is the charge for renting a canoe for 30 minutes?

  A customer is charged $8.50. How long did he use the canoe?

  A customer has $10 to spend. How long can she use a canoe?

  Suppose you were applying for a job at Sandy's. How would you answer these questions?

Problem 2.3 Solving Linear Equations

A. Rashida uses a graph of $c = 0.15t + 2.50$. Explain how to use the graph to estimate the answers to the manager's questions.

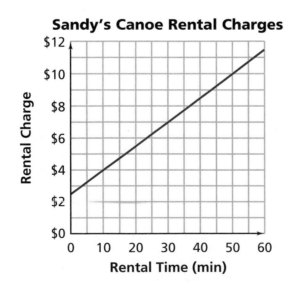

Sandy's Canoe Rental Charges

B. Rashida could use a table instead of a graph. Explain how to use a table to estimate answers to the questions.

C. Serena wants to find exact answers, not estimates. For the second question, she solves the linear equation $0.15t + 2.50 = 8.50$. She reasons as follows:

- If $0.15t + 2.50 = 8.50$, then $0.15t = 6.00$.
- If $0.15t = 6.00$, then $t = 40$.
- I check my answer by substituting 40 for t: $0.15(40) + 2.50 = 8.50$

Is Serena correct? How do you know?

D. For the third question, Rashida says, "She can use the canoe for 50 minutes if she has $10." Serena says there are other possibilities— for example, 45 minutes or 30 minutes. She says you can answer the question by solving the **inequality** $0.15t + 2.50 \leq 10$. This inequality represents the times for which the rental charge is *at most* $10.

1. Use a table, a graph, and the equation $0.15t + 2.50 = 10$ to find all of the times for which the inequality is true.

2. Express the solution as an inequality.

E. River Fun Paddle Boats competes with Sandy's. The equation $c = 4 + 0.10t$ gives the charge in dollars c for renting a paddle boat for t minutes.

1. A customer at River Fun is charged $9. How long did the customer use a paddle boat? Explain.

2. Suppose you want to spend $12 at most. How long could you use a paddle boat? Explain.

3. What is the charge to rent a paddle boat for 20 minutes? Explain.

ACE Homework starts on page 33.

2.4 Intersecting Linear Models

A resort area has two main attractions—the Big Fun amusement park and the Get Reel movie multiplex. The number of visitors to each attraction on a given day is related to the probability of rain.

This table gives attendance and rain-forecast data for several Saturdays.

Saturday Resort Attendance

Probability of Rain (%)	0	20	40	60	80	100
Big Fun Attendance	1,000	850	700	550	400	250
Get Reel Attendance	300	340	380	420	460	500

The same company owns both businesses. The managers want to be able to predict Saturday attendance at each attraction so they can assign their workers efficiently.

Problem 2.4 Intersecting Linear Models

A. Use the table to find a linear equation relating the probability of rain p to

   1. Saturday attendance A_B at Big Fun.

   2. Saturday attendance A_G at Get Reel.

B. Use your equations from Question A to answer these questions. Show your calculations and explain your reasoning.

   1. Suppose there is a 50% probability of rain this Saturday. What is the expected attendance at each attraction?

   2. Suppose 460 people visited Big Fun one Saturday. Estimate the probability of rain on that day.

   3. What probability of rain would give a predicted Saturday attendance of at least 360 people at Get Reel?

   4. Is there a probability of rain for which the predicted attendance is the same at both attractions? Explain.

 **ACE** Homework starts on page 33.

Applications

1. Below are some results from the bridge-thickness experiment.

Bridge-Thickness Experiment

Thickness (layers)	2	4	6	8
Breaking Weight (pennies)	15	30	50	65

   a. Plot the (*thickness, breaking weight*) data. Draw a line that models the pattern in the data.

   b. Find an equation for the line you drew.

   c. Use your equation to predict the breaking weights of paper bridges 3, 5, and 7 layers thick.

2. Which line do you think is a better model for the data? Explain.

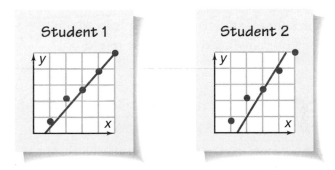

3. Copy each graph onto grid paper. Draw a line that fits each set of data as closely as possible. Describe the strategies you used.

Graph A   **Graph B**   **Graph C**

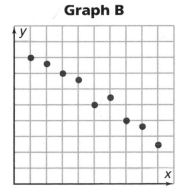
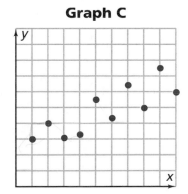

4. This table gives the average weights of purebred Chihuahuas from birth to 16 weeks.

Average Weights for Chihuahuas

Age (wk)	0	2	4	6	8	10	12	14	16
Weight (oz)	4	9	13	17.5	21.5	25	30	34	39

SOURCE: *The Complete Chihuahua Encyclopedia*

a. Graph the (*age, weight*) data. Draw a line that models the data pattern.

b. Write an equation of the form $y = mx + b$ for your line. Explain what the values of m and b tell you about this situation.

c. Use your equation to predict the average weight of Chihuahuas for odd-numbered ages from 1 to 15 weeks.

d. What average weight does your linear model predict for a Chihuahua that is 144 weeks old? Explain why this prediction is unlikely to be accurate.

5. U-Wash-It Car Wash did market research to determine how much to charge for a car wash. The company makes this table based on its findings.

Homework Help Online
PHSchool.com
For: Help with Exercise 5
Web Code: ape-1205

U-Wash-It Projections

Price per Wash	$0	$5	$10	$15	$20
Customers Expected per Day	100	80	65	45	20

a. Graph the (*price, expected customers*) data. Draw a line that models the data pattern.

b. Write an equation in the form $y = mx + b$ for your graph. Explain what the values of m and b tell you about this situation.

c. Use your equation to estimate the number of customers expected for prices of $2.50, $7.50, and $12.50.

6. Find the slope, y-intercept, and equation for each line.

a.
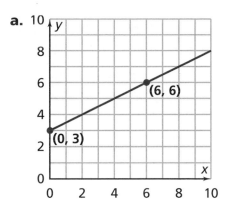

b.
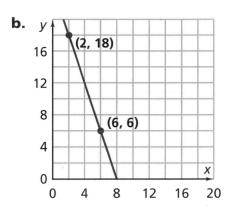

c.
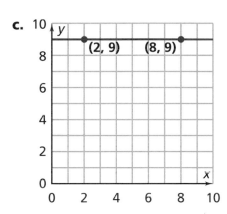

d.
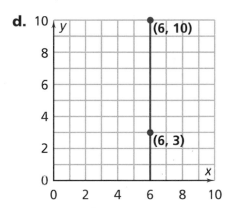

The relationships in Exercises 7–10 are linear.

7. a. A typical American baby weighs about 8 pounds at birth and gains about 1.5 pounds per month for the first year of life. What equation relates weight w in pounds to age a in months?

b. Can this model be used to predict weight at age 80? Explain.

8. Kaya buys a $20 phone card. She is charged $0.15 per minute for long-distance calls. What equation gives the value v left on her card after she makes t minutes of long-distance calls?

9. Dakota lives 1,500 meters from school. She leaves for school, walking at a speed of 60 meters per minute. Write an equation for her distance d in meters from school after she walks for t minutes.

10. A car can average 140 miles on 5 gallons of gasoline. Write an equation for the distance d in miles the car can travel on g gallons of gas.

11. Write a linear equation for each table relating x and y.

a.
x	0	3	6	10
y	2	8	14	22

b.
x	0	3	6	10
y	20	8	−4	−20

c.
x	2	4	6	8
y	5	8	11	14

d.
x	0	3	6	9
y	20	11	2	−7

For Exercises 12–17, find an equation for the line that satisfies the conditions.

12. Slope 4.2; y-intercept $(0, 3.4)$

13. Slope $\frac{2}{3}$; y-intercept $(0, 5)$

14. Slope 2; passes through $(4, 12)$

15. Passes through $(0, 15)$ and $(5, 3)$

16. Passes through $(-2, 2)$ and $(5, -4)$

17. Parallel to the line with equation $y = 15 - 2x$ and passes through $(3, 0)$

Go Online
PHSchool.com
For: Multiple-Choice Skills
Practice
Web Code: apa-1254

18. Write an equation for each line.

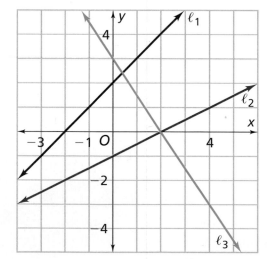

19. Anchee and Jonah earn weekly allowances for doing chores over the summer.

- Anchee's father pays her $5 each week.
- Jonah's mother paid him $20 at the beginning of the summer and now pays him $3 each week.

The relationships between number of weeks worked and dollars earned are shown in this graph.

Earnings From Chores

a. Which line represents Jonah's earnings? Which line represents Anchee's earnings? Explain.

b. Write two linear equations in the form $y = mx + b$ to show the relationships between Anchee's earnings and the number of weeks she works and between Jonah's earnings and the number of weeks he works.

c. What do the values of m and b in each equation tell about the relationship between the number of weeks and the dollars earned?

d. What do the values of m and b tell about each line?

For Exercises 20–23, do the following:

    a. Solve the equation. Show your steps.

    b. Graph the associated line (for example, for $5.5x + 32 = 57$, graph $y = 5.5x + 32$). Label the point that shows the solution.

20. $5.5x + 32 = 57$ **21.** $-24 = 4x - 12$

22. $5x - 51 = 24$ **23.** $74 = 53 - 7x$

24. At Water Works Amusement Park, the daily profit from the concession stands depends on the number of park visitors. The equation $p = 2.50v - 500$ gives the estimated profit p in dollars if v people visit the park. In parts (a)–(c), use a graph to estimate the answer. Then, find the answer by writing and solving an equation or inequality.

    a. For what number of visitors will the profit be about $2,000?

    b. One day 200 people visit the park. What is the approximate concession-stand profit for that day?

    c. For what number of visitors will the profit be at least $500?

25. The following formulas give the fare f in dollars that two bus companies charge for trips of d miles.

    Transcontinental: $f = 0.15d + 12$

    Intercity Express: $f = 5 + 0.20d$

    In parts (a)–(c), use a graph to estimate the answer. Then, find the answer by writing and solving an equation or inequality.

    a. For Transcontinental, how many miles is a trip that costs $99?

    b. For Intercity Express, how far can a person travel for a fare that is at most $99?

    c. Is there a distance for which the fare for the two bus lines is the same? If so, give the distance and the fare.

Solve each equation. Show the steps in your solutions.

26. $5x + 7 = 3x - 5$ **27.** $7 + 3x = 5x - 5$ **28.** $2.5x - 8 = 5x + 12$

Find at least three values of x for which the inequality is true.

29. $4x \leq 12$ **30.** $3x < 18$

31. $4x + 5 \leq 13$ **32.** $3x - 9 \leq 18$

33. Every Friday, the mechanic for Columbus Public Schools records the miles driven and the gallons of gas used for each school bus. One week, the mechanic records these data.

Data for Columbus Bus Fleet

Bus Number	1	2	3	4	5	6	7	8
Gas Used (gal)	5	8	12	15	18	20	22	25
Miles Driven	80	100	180	225	280	290	320	375

a. Write a linear equation that models the relationship between miles driven d and gallons of gas used g.

b. Use your equation to predict the number of miles such a bus could travel on 10 gallons of gas.

c. Use your equation to predict the number of gallons of gas required to drive such a bus 250 miles.

d. What do the values of m and b in your equation $d = mg + b$ tell about the fuel efficiency of the school bus fleet?

34. One of the most popular items at a farmers' market is sweet corn. This table shows relationships among the price for the corn, the demand for the corn (how much corn people want to buy), and the leftovers of corn (how much corn the market has at the end of the day).

Sweet Corn Supply and Demand

Price per Dozen	$1	$1.50	$2.00	$2.50	$3.00	$3.50
Demand (dozens)	200	175	140	120	80	60
Leftovers (dozens)	40	75	125	175	210	260

a. Why do you think the demand for corn decreases as the price goes up?

b. Why do you think the leftovers of corn increases as the price goes up?

c. Write a linear equation that models the relationship between demand d and price p.

d. Write a linear equation that models the relationship between leftovers ℓ and price p.

e. Use graphs to estimate the price for which the leftovers equals the demand. Then, find the price by solving symbolically.

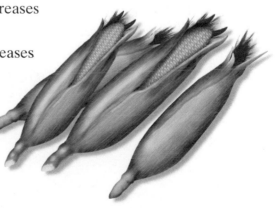

Connections

35. Tell whether each table represents a linear relationship. Explain.

a.

x	2	4	6	8	10	12	14
y	0	1	2	3	4	5	6

b.

x	1	2	3	4	5	6	7
y	0	3	8	15	24	35	48

c.

x	1	4	6	7	10	12	16
y	2	−1	−3	−4	−7	−9	−13

36. For parts (a)–(d), copy the table. Then, use the equation to complete the table. Tell whether the relationship is linear. Explain.

a. $y = -3x - 8$

x	−5	−2	1	4
y				

b. $y = 4(x - 7) + 6$

x	−3	0	3	6
y				

c. $y = x(3x + 2)$

x	−3	0	3	6
y				

d. $y = 4 - 3x$

x	−3	0	3	10
y				

Copy each pair of numbers in Exercises 37–42. Insert <, >, or = to make a true statement.

37. $-5 \ \blacksquare \ 3$

38. $\dfrac{2}{3} \ \blacksquare \ \dfrac{1}{2}$

39. $\dfrac{9}{12} \ \blacksquare \ \dfrac{3}{4}$

40. $3.009 \ \blacksquare \ 3.1$

41. $\dfrac{-2}{3} \ \blacksquare \ \dfrac{-1}{2}$

42. $-4.25 \ \blacksquare \ -2.45$

43. Madeline sets a copy machine to enlarge by a factor of 150%. She then uses the machine to copy a polygon. Write an equation that relates the perimeter of the polygon after the enlargement *a* to the perimeter before the enlargement *b*.

For Exercises 44–52, evaluate the expression without using a calculator.

44. $-15 + (-7)$ **45.** $-7 - 15$ **46.** $-7 - (-15)$

47. $-15 + 7$ **48.** $-20 \div 5$ **49.** $-20 \div (-5)$

50. $20 \div (-4)$ **51.** $-20 \div (-2.5)$ **52.** $-20 \cdot (-2.5)$

53. You can express the slope of a line in different ways. The slope of the line below is $\frac{6}{10}$, or 0.6. You can also say the slope is 60% because the rise is 60% of the run.

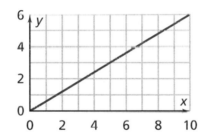

These numbers represent slopes of lines.

$\frac{-4}{-2}$ 60% $\frac{4}{4}$ 1.5   150%   200%

a. Which numbers represent the same slope?

b. Which number represents the greatest slope? Which represents the least slope?

54. Consider the following stories and the graphs.

   a. Match each story with a graph. Tell how you would label the axes. Explain how each part of the story is represented in the graph.

Story 1 A parachutist is taken up in a plane. After he jumps, the wind blows him off course. He ends up tangled in the branches of a tree.

Story 2 Ella puts some money in the bank. She leaves it there to earn interest for several years. Then one day, she withdraws half of the money in the account.

Story 3 Gerry has a big pile of gravel to spread on his driveway. On the first day, he moves half of the gravel from the pile to his driveway. The next day he is tired and moves only half of what is left. The third day he again moves half of what is left in the pile. He continues in this way until the pile has almost disappeared.

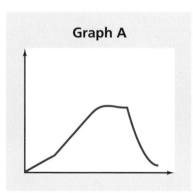

Graph A

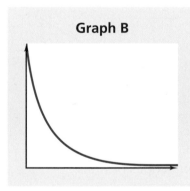

Graph B

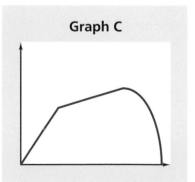

Graph C

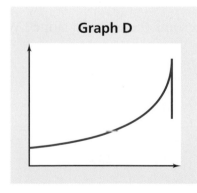

Graph D

   b. One of the graphs does not match a story. Make up your own story for that graph.

55. The figures below are similar.

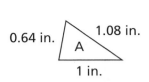 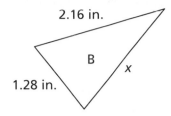

a. Find x.

b. What is the scale factor from Triangle A to Triangle B?

c. What is the scale factor from Triangle B to Triangle A?

d. How are the scale factors in parts (b) and (c) related?

Extensions

56. A bridge-painting company uses the formula $C = 5{,}000 + 150L$ to estimate painting costs. C is the cost in dollars, and L is the length of the bridge in feet. To make a profit, the company increases a cost estimate by 20% to arrive at a bid price. For example, if the cost estimate is $10,000, the bid price will be $12,000.

a. Find bid prices for bridges 100 feet, 200 feet, and 400 feet long.

b. Write a formula relating the final bid price to bridge length.

c. Use your formula to find bid prices for bridges 150 feet, 300 feet, and 450 feet long.

d. How would your formula change if the markup for profit was 15% instead of 20%?

57. Recall that Custom Steel Products builds beams from steel rods. Here is a 7-foot beam.

7-foot beam made from 27 rods

a. Which of these formulas represents the relationship between beam length ℓ and number of rods r?

$r = 3\ell$ $\qquad\qquad\qquad\qquad$ $r = \ell + (\ell - 1) + 2\ell$

$r = 4(\ell - 1) + 3$ $\qquad\qquad\quad$ $r = 4\ell - 1$

b. How might you have reasoned to come up with each formula?

58. Recall that Custom Steel Products uses steel rods to make staircase frames. Here are staircase frames with 1, 2, and 3 steps.

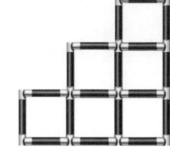

| 1 step
made from 4 rods | 2 steps
made from 10 rods | 3 steps
made from 18 rods |

Which of these formulas represents the relationship between the number of steps n and number of rods r?

$r = n^2 + 3n$ $r = n(n + 3)$

$r = n^2 + 3$ $r = (n + 3)n$

Custom Steel Products builds cubes out of square steel plates measuring 1 foot on a side. At right is a 1-foot cube. Use this information for Exercises 59–61.

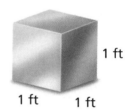

1 ft

1 ft   1 ft

59. How many square plates are needed to make a 1-foot cube?

60. Multiple Choice Suppose CSP wants to triple the dimensions of the cube. How many times the number of plates in the original cube will they need for this larger cube?

A. 2   **B.** 3   **C.** 4   **D.** 9

61. Multiple Choice Suppose CSP triples the dimensions of the original cube. How many times the volume of the original cube is the volume of the new cube?

F. 8   **G.** 9   **H.** 27   **J.** 81

62. At Yvonne's Auto Detailing, car washes cost $5 for any time up to 10 minutes, plus $0.40 per minute after that. The managers at Yvonne's are trying to agree on a formula for calculating the cost c for a t-minute car wash.

a. Sid thinks $c = 0.4t + 5$ is correct. Is he right?

b. Tina proposes the formula $c = 0.4(t - 10) + 5$. Is she right?

c. Jamal told Tina her formula could be simplified to $c = 0.4t + 1$. Is he right?

63. Write an equation for each relationship.

a. One taxi company charges $1.50 for the first 2 miles of any trip, and then $1.20 for each mile after that. How is the taxi *fare* related to the *distance* of a trip?

b. An airport offers free parking for 30 minutes and then charges $2.00 for each hour after that. How is the *price* for parking related to the *time* a car is parked?

c. A local cinema makes $6.50 on each ticket sold. However, it has operating expenses of $750 per day. How is *daily profit* related to *number of tickets* sold?

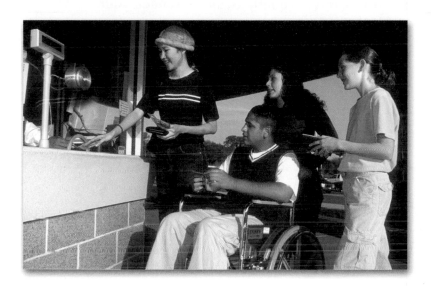

d. Rush Computer Repair sends technicians to businesses to fix computers. They charge a fixed fee of $50, plus $50 per hour. How is total *cost* for a repair related to *time* the repair takes?

Mathematical Reflections 2

In this investigation, you learned how to find linear models for data patterns. You also developed skill in writing linear equations, practiced translating verbal descriptions into linear equations, and extended your knowledge of solving linear equations.

Think about your answers to these questions. Discuss your ideas with other students and your teacher. Then write a summary of your findings in your notebook.

1. What are the advantages of using a linear model for a set of data?

2. How would you find the equation for a linear relationship
   a. from a verbal description?
   b. from a table of values?
   c. from a graph?

3. What strategies can you use to solve a linear equation such as
   a. $500 = 245 + 5x$?
   b. $500 + 3x = 245 + 5x$?

Investigation 3

Inverse Variation

In Investigation 1, you discovered that the relationship between bridge thickness and bridge strength is approximately linear. You also found that the relationship between bridge length and bridge strength is not linear. In this investigation, you will explore other nonlinear relationships.

3.1 Rectangles With Fixed Area

In recent years, the populations of many small towns have declined as residents move to large cities for jobs. The town of Roseville has developed a plan to attract new residents. The town is offering free lots of land to "homesteaders" who are willing to build houses. Each lot is rectangular and has an area of 21,800 square feet. The lengths and widths of the lots vary.

Getting Ready for Problem 3.1

- What are some possible dimensions for a rectangular lot with an area of 21,800 square feet?

In Problem 3.1, you will look at patterns in length and width values for rectangles with fixed area.

Problem 3.1 Relating Length and Width

A. 1. Copy and complete this table.

Rectangles With Area 24 in.²

Length (in.)	1	2	3	4	5	6	7	8
Width (in.)	▧	▧	▧	▧	▧	▧	▧	▧

2. Plot your data on a grid like the one below. Then, draw a line or curve that seems to model the pattern in the data.

Rectangles With Area 24 in.²

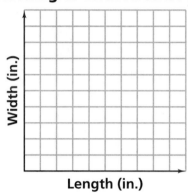

Length (in.)

3. Describe the pattern of change in the width as the length increases. Is the relationship between length and width linear?

4. Write an equation that shows how the width w depends on the length ℓ for rectangles with an area of 24 square inches.

B. Now consider rectangles with an area of 32 square inches.

1. Write an equation for the relationship between the length ℓ and the width w.

2. Graph your equation. Show lengths from 1 to 15 inches.

C. Compare your equations. How are they similar? How are they different?

D. Compare your graphs. How are they similar? How are they different?

ACE **Homework starts on page 53.**

3.2 Bridging the Distance

The relationship between length and width for rectangles with a fixed area is not linear. It is an example of an important type of nonlinear pattern called an **inverse variation.**

The word "inverse" suggests that as one variable increases in value, the other variable decreases in value. However, the meaning of *inverse variation* is more specific than this. The relationship between two non-zero variables, *x* and *y*, is an inverse variation if

$$y = \frac{k}{x}, \text{ or } xy = k$$

where *k* is a constant that is not 0. The value of *k* is determined by the specific relationship.

> *How are the equations* $y = \frac{k}{x}$ *and* $xy = k$ *related?*

> *For the same* x-*value, will the two equations give different* y-*values?*

Inverse variation occurs in many situations. For example, consider the table and graph below. They show the (*bridge length, breaking weight*) data collected by a group of students.

Bridge Experiment Data

Length (in.)	Breaking Weight (pennies)
4	41
6	26
8	19
9	17
10	15

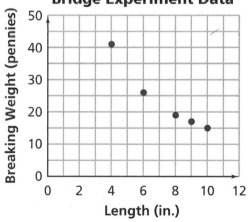

Bridge Experiment Data

Getting Ready for Problem

- Describe a curve that models the pattern in the data above.
- What value of *k* can you use to model these data with an inverse variation equation? Write the equation.
- In your equation, why does the value of *y* decrease as the value of *x* increases?
- What happens to the value of *y* as the value of *x* gets close to 0? Why is that a reasonable pattern for the bridge experiment?

Mr. Cordova lives in Detroit, Michigan. He often travels to Baltimore, Maryland, to visit his grandfather. The trip is 500 miles each way. Here are his notes for his trips to Baltimore last year.

Date	Notes	Travel Time
February 15	Traveled by plane.	1.5 hours
May 22	Drove.	10 hours
July 3	Drove. Stopped for repairs.	14 hours
November 23	Flew. Flight delayed.	4 hours
December 23	Took overnight train.	18 hours

A. 1. Calculate the average speed in miles per hour for each trip. Record the results in a table like this.

Cordova's Baltimore Trips

Travel Time (hr)	■	■	■	■	■
Average Speed (mph)	■	■	■	■	■

2. Plot the data. Draw a line or curve that models the data pattern. Describe the pattern of change in average speed as travel time increases.

3. Write an equation for the relationship between travel time t and average speed s.

4. Use your equation to find the average speed for 500-mile trips that take 6 hours, 8 hours, 12 hours, and 16 hours.

5. Add the (*travel time, average speed*) data from part (4) to your graph. Do the new points fit the graph model you sketched for the original data?

B. The Cordova family is planning a trip to Mackinac Island (mak uh naw) near the upper peninsula of Michigan. Mr. Cordova does some calculations to see how the travel time will change if the family drives at different average speeds.

Travel Times for Different Speeds

Average Speed (mi/h)	30	40	50	60	70
Travel Time (hr)	10	7.5	6	5	4.3

  1. How far is it from Detroit to Mackinac Island?

  2. What equation relates travel time *t* to average speed *s*?

  3. Describe the pattern of change in the travel time as the average speed increases. How would that pattern appear in a graph of the data? How is it shown by your equation?

  4. Predict the travel times if the Cordovas drive at average speeds of 45 miles per hour and 65 miles per hour.

C. Suppose Mr. Cordova decides to aim for an average speed of 50 miles per hour for the trip to Mackinac Island.

  1. Make a table and graph to show how the distance traveled will increase as time passes. Show times from when the family leaves home to when they reach their destination.

  2. Write an equation for the distance *d* the family travels in *t* hours.

  3. Describe the pattern of change in the distance as time passes.

  4. Compare the (*time, distance traveled*) graph and equation with the (*time, average speed*) graphs and equations in Questions A and B.

ACE Homework starts on page 53.

3.3 Average Cost

The science teachers at Everett Middle School want to take their eighth-graders on an overnight field trip to a nature center. It costs $750 to rent the center facilities. The school budget does not provide funds to rent the nature center, so students must pay a fee. The trip will cost $3 per student if all 250 students go. However, the teachers know it is unlikely that all students can go. They want to find the cost per student for any number of students.

Problem 3.3 Inverse Variation Patterns

A. 1. Write an equation relating the cost *c* per student to the number of students *n*.

   2. Use your equation to make a graph showing how the cost per student changes as the number of students increases.

B. 1. Find the change in the cost per student as the number of students increases from

   a. 10 to 20   **b.** 100 to 110   **c.** 200 to 210

   2. How do your results show that the relationship between the number of students and the cost per student is not linear?

C. 1. Find the change in the per-student cost as the number of students increases from

   a. 20 to 40   **b.** 40 to 80   **c.** 80 to 160

   2. Describe the pattern in your results. Explain how your equation from Question A shows this pattern.

D. The science teachers decide to charge $5 per student for the trip. They will use any extra money to buy science equipment for the school.

   1. Write an equation for the amount *a* the teachers will collect if *n* students go on the trip.

   2. Sketch a graph of the relationship.

   3. Is this a linear relationship or an inverse variation? Explain.

ACE Homework starts on page 53.

Applications

1. Consider rectangles with an area of 16 square inches.

   a. Copy and complete the table.

Rectangles With an Area of 16 in.²

Length (in.)	1	2	3	4	5	6	7	8
Width (in.)	▪	▪	▪	▪	▪	▪	▪	▪

   b. Make a graph of the data.

   c. Describe the pattern of change in width as length increases.

   d. Write an equation that shows how the width w depends on the length ℓ. Is the relationship linear?

2. Consider rectangles with an area of 20 square inches.

   a. Make a table of length and width data for at least five rectangles.

   b. Make a graph of your data.

   c. Write an equation that shows how the width w depends on the length ℓ. Is the relationship linear?

   d. Compare and contrast the graphs in this exercise and in Exercise 1.

   e. Compare and contrast the equations in this exercise and in Exercise 1.

3. A student collected these data from the bridge-length experiment.

Bridge-Length Experiment

Length (in.)	4	6	8	9	10
Breaking Weight (pennies)	24	16	13	11	9

   a. Find an inverse variation equation that models these data.

   b. Explain how your equation shows that breaking weight decreases as length increases. Is this pattern reasonable for this situation? Explain.

For Exercises 4–7, tell whether the relationship between x and y is an inverse variation. If it is, write an equation for the relationship.

4.

x	1	2	3	4	5	6	7	8	9	10
y	10	9	8	7	6	5	4	3	2	1

5.

x	1	2	3	4	5	6	7	8	9	10
y	48	24	16	12	9.6	8	6.8	6	5.3	4.8

6.

x	2	3	5	8	10	15	20	25	30	40
y	50	33	20	12.5	10	6.7	5	4	3.3	2.5

7.

x	0	1	2	3	4	5	6	7	8	9
y	100	81	64	49	36	25	16	9	4	1

8. A marathon is a 26.2-mile race. The best marathon runners can complete the race in a little more than 2 hours.

   a. Make a table and graph that show how the average running speed for a marathon changes as the time increases. Show times from 2 to 8 hours in 1-hour intervals.

   b. Write an equation for the relationship between time t and average running speed s for a marathon.

   c. Tell how the average running speed changes as the time increases from 2 hours to 3 hours. From 3 hours to 4 hours. From 4 hours to 5 hours.

   d. How do the answers for part (c) show that the relationship between average running speed and time is not linear?

9. On one day of a charity bike ride, the route covers 50 miles. Individual riders cover this distance at different average speeds.

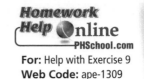

For: Help with Exercise 9
Web Code: ape-1309

  a. Make a table and a graph that show how the riding time changes as the average speed increases. Show speed values from 4 to 20 miles per hour in intervals of 4 miles per hour.

  b. Write an equation for the relationship between the riding time t and average speed s.

  c. Tell how the riding time changes as the average speed increases from 4 to 8 miles per hour. From 8 to 12 miles per hour. From 12 to 16 miles per hour.

  d. How do the answers for part (c) show that the relationship between average speed and time is not linear?

10. Students in Mr. Einstein's science class complain about the length of his tests. He argues that a test with more questions is better for students because each question is worth fewer points. All of Mr. Einstein's tests are worth 100 points. Each question is worth the same number of points.

  a. Make a table and a graph that show how the number of points per question changes as the number of questions increases. Show point values for 2 to 20 questions in intervals of 2.

  b. Write an equation for the relationship between the number of questions n and the points per question p.

  c. Tell how the points per question changes as the number of questions increases from 2 to 4. From 4 to 6. From 6 to 8. From 8 to 10.

  d. How do the answers for part (c) show that the relationship between the number of questions and the points per question is not linear?

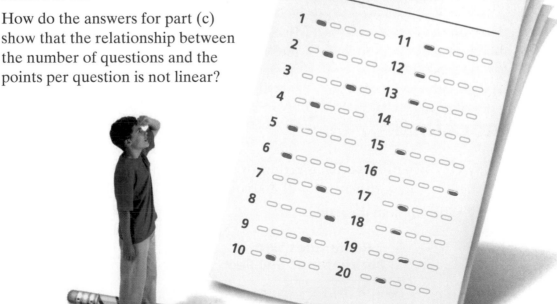

11. Testers drive eight vehicles 200 miles on a test track at the same speed. The table shows the amount of fuel each vehicle uses.

Fuel-Efficiency Test

Vehicle Type	Fuel Used (gal)
Large Truck	20
Large SUV	18
Limousine	16
Large Sedan	12
Small Truck	10
Sports Car	12
Compact Car	7
Sub-Compact Car	5

a. Find the fuel efficiency in miles per gallon for each vehicle.

b. Make a graph of the (*fuel used, miles per gallon*) data. Describe the pattern of change shown in the graph.

c. Write a formula for calculating the fuel efficiency based on the fuel used for a 200-mile test drive.

d. Tell how the fuel efficiency changes as the amount of fuel used increases from 5 to 10 gallons. From 10 to 15 gallons. From 15 to 20 gallons.

e. How do the answers for part (d) show that the relationship between the fuel used and the fuel efficiency is not linear?

Connections

12. Suppose the town of Roseville is giving away lots with perimeters of 500 feet, rather than with areas of 21,800 square feet.

a. Copy and complete this table.

**Rectangles With a
Perimeter of 500 Feet**

Length (ft)	■	■	■	■	■
Width (ft)	■	■	■	■	■

b. Make a graph of the (*length, width*) data. Draw a line or curve that models the data pattern.

c. Describe the pattern of change in width as length increases.

d. Write an equation for the relationship between length and width. Is this a linear relationship? Explain.

A number *b* is the additive inverse of the number *a* if *a* + *b* = 0.
For example, −5 is the additive inverse of 5 because 5 + (−5) = 0.
For Exercises 13–18, find the additive inverse of each number.

For: Multiple-Choice Skills Practice
Web Code: apa-1354

13. 2

14. $-\frac{6}{2}$

15. 2.5

16. −2.11

17. $\frac{7}{3}$

18. $\frac{3}{7}$

19. On a number line, graph each number in Exercises 13–18 and its additive inverse. Describe any patterns you see.

A number *b* is the multiplicative inverse of the number *a* if *ab* = 1. For
example, $\frac{3}{2}$ is the multiplicative inverse of $\frac{2}{3}$ because $\left(\frac{2}{3}\right)\left(\frac{3}{2}\right) = 1$. For
Exercises 20–25, find the multiplicative inverse of each number.

20. 2

21. −2

22. 0.5

23. 4

24. $\frac{3}{4}$

25. $\frac{5}{3}$

26. On a number line, graph each number in Exercises 20–25 and its multiplicative inverse. Describe any patterns you see.

Jamar takes a 10-point history quiz each week. Here are his scores on the
first five quizzes: 8, 9, 6, 7, 10. Use this information for Exercises 27–28.

27. Multiple Choice What is Jamar's average quiz score?

A. 6   **B.** 7

C. 8   **D.** 9

28. a. Jamar misses the next quiz and gets a 0. What is his average after six quizzes?

b. After 20 quizzes, Jamar's average is 8. He gets a 0 on the 21st quiz. What is his average after 21 quizzes?

c. Why did a score of 0 have a different effect on the average when it was the sixth score than when it was the 21st score?

29. Suppose a car travels at a speed of 60 miles per hour. The equation $d = 60t$ represents the relationship between the time t in hours and the distance d driven in miles. This relationship is an example of a *direct variation*. A relationship between variables x and y is a direct variation if it can be expressed as $y = kx$, where k is a constant.

    a. Find two relationships in this unit that are direct variations. Give the equation for each relationship.

    b. For each relationship from part (a), find the ratio of the dependent variable to the independent variable. How is the ratio related to k in the general equation?

    c. Suppose the relationship between x and y is a direct variation. How do y-values change as the x-values increase? How does this pattern of change appear in a graph of the relationship?

    d. Compare direct variation and inverse variation. Be sure to discuss the graphs and equations for these types of relationships.

Solve the equation using a symbolic method. Then, describe how the solution can be found by using a graph and a table.

30. $5x - 28 = -3$ **31.** $10 - 3x = 7x - 10$

For Exercises 32–34, find the equation of the line with the given information.

32. slope $-\frac{1}{2}$, y-intercept $(0, 5)$

33. slope 3, passes through the point $(2, 2)$

34. passes through the points $(5, 2)$ and $(1, 10)$

35. Find the equation for the line below.

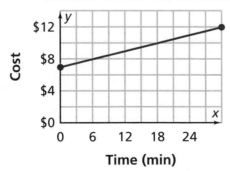

Al Jabr's Self-Serve Wash

36. Suppose 6 cans of tomato juice cost $3.20. Find the cost for

    a. 1 can   **b.** 10 cans   **c.** n cans

For Exercises 37–39, tell which store offers the better buy. Explain your choice.

37. *Gus's Groceries*: Tomatoes are 6 for $4.00
Super Market: Tomatoes are 8 for $4.60

38. *Gus's Groceries*: Cucumbers are 4 for $1.75
Super Market: Cucumbers are 5 for $2.00

39. *Gus's Groceries*: Apples are 6 for $3.00
Super Market: Apples are 5 for $2.89

Extensions

40. This net folds up to make a rectangular prism.

   a. What is the volume of the prism?

   b. Suppose the dimensions of the shaded face are doubled. The other dimensions are adjusted so that the volume remains the same. What are the dimensions of the new prism?

   c. Which prism has the smaller surface area, the original prism or the prism from part (b)? Explain.

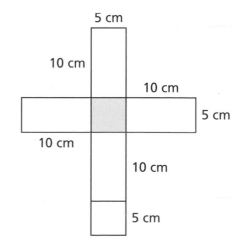

41. Ms. Singh drives 40 miles to her sister's house. Her average speed is 20 miles per hour. On her way home, her average speed is 40 miles per hour. What is her average speed for the round trip?

42. The drama club members at Henson Middle School are planning their spring show. They decide to charge $4.50 per ticket. They estimate their expenses for the show at $150.

    a. Write an equation for the relationship between the number of tickets sold and the club's total profit.

    b. Make a table to show how the profit changes as the ticket sales increase from 0 to 500 in intervals of 50.

    c. Make a graph of the (*tickets sold, total profit*) data.

    d. Add a column (or row) to your table to show the per-ticket profit for each number of tickets sold. For example, for 200 tickets, the total profit is $750, so the per-ticket profit is $750 ÷ 200, or $3.75.

    e. Make a graph of the (*tickets sold, per-ticket profit*) data.

    f. How are the patterns of change for the (*tickets sold, total profit*) data and (*tickets sold, per-ticket profit*) data similar? How are they different? How are the similarities and differences shown in the tables and graphs of each relationship?

For Exercises 43–45, find the value of c for which both ordered pairs satisfy the same inverse variation. Then, write an equation for the relationship.

43. $(3, 16), (12, c)$ **44.** $(3, 9), (4, c)$ **45.** $(3, 4), (4, c)$

46. Multiple Choice The force acting on a falling object due to gravity is related to the mass and acceleration of the object. For a fixed force F, the relationship between mass m and acceleration a is an inverse variation. Which equation shows the relationship between F, m, and a?

    A. $F = ma$ **B.** $m = Fa$ **C.** $\frac{m}{F} = a$ **D.** $\frac{m}{a} = F$

47. Multiple Choice Suppose the time t in the equation $d = rt$ is held constant. What happens to the distance d as the rate r increases?

    F. d decreases.   **G.** d increases.

    H. d stays constant.   **J.** There is not enough information.

48. Multiple Choice Suppose the distance d in the equation $d = rt$ is held constant. What happens to the time t as the rate r increases?

    A. t decreases.   **B.** t increases.

    C. t stays constant.   **D.** There is not enough information.

Mathematical Reflections 3

In this investigation, you explored several examples of inverse variations and looked for patterns in the tables, graphs, and equations of these relationships. These questions will help you summarize what you have learned.

Think about your answers to these questions. Discuss your ideas with other students and your teacher. Then, write a summary of your findings in your notebook.

1. Suppose the relationship between variables x and y is an inverse variation.

    a. How do the values of y change as values of x increase?

    b. Describe the pattern in a graph of (x, y) values.

    c. Describe the equation that relates the values of x and y.

2. How is an inverse relationship similar to a linear relationship? How is it different?

Looking Back and Looking Ahead

Unit Review

While working on the problems in this unit, you extended your skill in writing equations to express linear relationships. You also learned about a type of nonlinear relationship called an inverse variation. You used inverse and linear relationships to solve problems and make predictions.

For: Vocabulary Review Puzzle
Web Code: apj-1051

Use Your Understanding:
Linear and Inverse Variation

Test your understanding of linear relationships and inverse variations by solving the following problems about a recreation area that has a playground, hiking trails, amusement rides, and a small farm.

1. This table shows the growth of one pig that was raised on the farm.

Average Growth of Properly-Fed Pig

Age (mo)	0	1	2	3	4	5	6
Weight (lb)	3	48	92	137	182	228	273

SOURCE: Your 4-H Market Hog Project, Iowa State University.

   a. Make a graph of the (*age, weight*) data. Draw a line that seems to fit the data pattern.

   b. Find a linear equation in the form $y = mx + b$ for your line from part (a).

   c. What do the values of m and b in your equation tell you about the growth of the pig?

   d. Use your equation to estimate the pig's weight at 3.5 months and at 7 months.

2. One group of students suspects that farm animals eat less when the weather is warmer. They ask the farm staff to keep a record of what an adult goat eats on days with different average temperatures.

Food Consumption for a Goat

Average Daily Temperature (°F)	30	40	45	55	60	75	85	90
Food Eaten (kg)	3.9	3.6	3.4	3.0	2.7	2.5	2.2	1.9

a. Make a graph of the (*temperature, food eaten*) data. Draw a line that seems to fit the data pattern.

b. Find a linear equation in the form $y = mx + b$ for your line from part (a).

c. What do the values of m and b tell you about the relationship between temperature and the goat's food consumption?

d. Use your equation to predict how much the goat would eat on a day with an average temperature of 50°F. On a day with an average temperature of 70°F.

3. A small train gives visitors rides around the park on a 5,000-meter track. The time the trip takes varies. When many people are waiting in line, the drivers go quickly. When there are fewer people waiting, they go more slowly.

a. Sketch a graph showing how the average speed (in meters per minute) changes as the trip time (in minutes) increases.

b. For what parts of your graph are the predicted speeds realistic? Explain.

c. Write an equation relating the average speed s to the trip time t.

d. Write several sentences explaining as accurately as possible how average speed changes as trip time changes. In particular, describe the type of variation involved in this relationship.

Explain Your Reasoning

In this unit, you learned how to use models of linear relationships and inverse variations to solve a variety of problems. When you present work based on these relationships, you should be able to justify your calculations and conclusions.

4. How do you decide when a data pattern can be modeled well by a linear equation in the form $y = mx + b$? How will the values m and b relate to the data pattern?

5. How are the data patterns, graphs, and equations for the inverse variations you studied similar to and different from those modeled by linear equations?

6. How can a graph or equation model for a relationship be used to solve practical problems?

7. What limitations do mathematical models have as problem-solving tools?

Look Ahead

The work you did with linear relationships and inverse variations in this unit will be useful in many upcoming *Connected Mathematics* units and in the algebra and calculus courses you take in the future. As you progress through high school and college, you will see that linear and inverse relationships have applications in science, economics, business, technology, and many other fields of study.

English/Spanish Glossary

A

additive inverses Two numbers, a and b, that satisfy the equation $a + b = 0$. For example, 3 and -3 are additive inverses, and $\frac{1}{2}$ and $-\frac{1}{2}$ are additive inverses.

inversos aditivos Dos números, a y b, que cumplen con la ecuación $a + b = 0$. Por ejemplo, 3 y -3 son inversos aditivos, y $\frac{1}{2}$ y $-\frac{1}{2}$ son inversos aditivos.

I

inequality A statement that two quantities are not equal. The symbols $>$, $<$, $\geq$, and $\leq$ are used to express inequalities. For example, if a and b are two quantities, then "a is greater than b" is written as $a > b$, and "a is less than b" is written as $a < b$. The statement $a \geq b$ means "a is greater than or equal to b." The statement $a \leq b$ means that "a is less than or equal to b."

desigualdad Enunciado que dice que dos cantidades no son iguales. Los signos $>$, $<$, $\geq$, y $\leq$ se usan para expresar desigualdades. Por ejemplo, si a y b son dos cantidades, entonces "a es mayor que b", se escribe $a > b$, y "a es menor que b" se escribe $a < b$. El enunciado $a \geq b$ quiere decir "a es mayor que o igual a b." El enunciado $a \leq b$ quiere decir "a es menor que o igual a b."

inverse variation A nonlinear relationship in which the product of two variables is constant. An inverse variation can be represented by an equation of the form $y = \frac{k}{x}$, or $xy = k$, where k is a constant. In an inverse variation, the values of one variable decrease as the values of the other variable increase. In the bridge-length experiment, the relationship between length and breaking weight was an inverse variation.

variación inversa Una relación no lineal en la que el producto de dos variables es constante. Una variación inversa se puede representar por una ecuación de la forma $y = \frac{k}{x}$, ó $xy = k$, donde k es una constante. En una variación inversa, los valores de una variable disminuyen a medida que los valores de la otra variable aumentan. En el experimento de la longitud de los puentes, la relación entre la longitud y el peso de colapso era una variación inversa.

L

linear relationship A relationship in which there is a constant rate of change between two variables. A linear relationship can be represented by a straight-line graph and by an equation of the form $y = mx + b$. In the equation, m is the slope of the line, and b is the y-intercept.

relación líneal Una relación en la que hay una tasa de cambio constante entre dos variables. Una relación lineal se puede representar por una gráfica de línea recta y por una ecuación de la forma $y = mx + b$. En la ecuación, m es la pendiente de la recta y b es el intercepto y.

mathematical model An equation or a graph that describes, at least approximately, the relationship between two variables. In this unit, mathematical models are made by acquiring data, plotting the data points, and, when the points showed a pattern, finding an equation or curve that fits the trend in the data. A mathematical model allows you to make reasonable guesses for values between and sometimes beyond the data points.

modelo matemático Una ecuación o una gráfica que describe, al menos approximadamente, la relación entre dos variables. En esta unidad, los modelos matemáticos se hacen obteniendo datos, trazando los puntos de los datos y, cuando los puntos muestran un patrón, hallando la ecuación o curva que muestra la tendencia de los datos. Un modelo matemático permite hacer estimaciones razonables para los valores entre y, a veces, fuera de los puntos de los datos.

multiplicative inverses Two numbers, a and b, that satisfy the equation $ab = 1$. For example, 3 and $\frac{1}{3}$ are multiplicative inverses, and $-\frac{1}{2}$ and -2 are multiplicative inverses.

inversos multiplicativos Dos números, a y b, que cumplen con la ecuación $ab = 1$. Por ejemplo, 3 y $\frac{1}{3}$ son inversos multiplicativos, y $-\frac{1}{2}$ y -2 son inversos multiplicativos.

Index

Acknowledgments

Team Credits

The people who made up the **Connected Mathematics 2** team —representing editorial, editorial services, design services, and production services— are listed below. Bold type denotes core team members.

Leora Adler, Judith Buice, Kerry Cashman, Patrick Culleton, Sheila DeFazio, Katie Hallahan, Richard Heater, **Barbara Hollingdale, Jayne Holman,** Karen Holtzman, **Etta Jacobs,** Christine Lee, Carolyn Lock, Catherine Maglio, **Dotti Marshall,** Rich McMahon, Eve Melnechuk, Kristin Mingrone, Terri Mitchell, **Marsha Novak,** Irene Rubin, Donna Russo, Robin Samper, Siri Schwartzman, **Nancy Smith,** Emily Soltanoff, **Mark Tricca,** Paula Vergith, Roberta Warshaw, Helen Young

Additional Credits

Diana Bonfilio, Mairead Reddin, Michael Torocsik, nSight, Inc.

Technical Illustration

WestWords, Inc.

Cover Design:

tom white.images

Photos

2 t, Jay S. Simon/Getty Images, Inc.; **2 b,** Jeff Greenberg/Alamy; **3,** Photodisc/Getty Images, Inc.; **5,** Kaluzny-Thatcher/Getty Images, Inc.; **7,** Javier Larrea/AGE Fotostock; **9,** Simon DesRochers/Masterfile; **14,** Jay S. Simon/Getty Images, Inc.; **16,** Richard Haynes; **21,** Richard Haynes; **26,** Galen Rowell/Corbis; **31,** Jeff Greenberg/Alamy; **34,** Ron Kimball/Ron Kimball Stock; **37,** PictureQuest; **41,** Richard Haynes; **42,** SuperStock, Inc./SuperStock; **45,** Bob Daemmrich/PhotoEdit; **50,** Yellow Dog Productions/Getty Images, Inc.; **51,** Macduff Everton/Corbis; **54,** AP Photo/Keystone/Steffen Schmidt; **55,** Richard Haynes; **57,** Richard Haynes; **59,** Dennis MacDonald/PhotoEdit; **63,** Photodisc/Getty Images, Inc.

Data Sources

The information on the average weights for chihuahuas on page 34 is from The Complete Chihuahua Encyclopedia by Hilary Harmar. Published by Arco Reprints, 1973.
The information on the average growth of pigs on page 62 is from "Your 4H Hog Market Project," Iowa State University, University Extension, January, 1922.